LONGSHIPS LIGHTHOUSE

ELISABETH STANBROOK

TWELVEHEADS PRESS

TRURO 2016

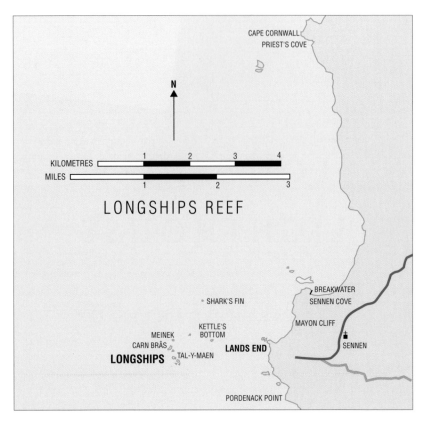

CAPE CORNWALL
PRIEST'S COVE

N

KILOMETRES 1 2 3 4
MILES 1 2 3

LONGSHIPS REEF

BREAKWATER
SHARK'S FIN   SENNEN COVE

MAYON CLIFF
KETTLE'S
MEINEK   BOTTOM
CARN BRÂS   SENNEN
LONGSHIPS TAL-Y-MAEN LANDS END

PORDENACK POINT

TWELVEHEADS PRESS

First published in 2016 by
Twelveheads Press, Truro, Cornwall.
ISBN 978 0 906294 86 4
British Library Cataloguing-in-Publication Data.
A catalogue record for this book is available
from the British Library.

Typeset in Albertus and Frutiger

Cover: Longships lighthouse. *Tim Stevens*
Back Cover:
Longships against a setting sun. *Tim Stevens*

CONTENTS

INTRODUCTION

Land's End is an iconic landscape, alluring and full of historic interest. Its surrounding Atlantic Ocean can be a turbulent mass of clashing currents and racing tides, with howling winds and torrential rain or swirling mist. About 2 km beyond the dramatic cliff edges are treacherous rocky outcrops, some of which become partially concealed with each rising tide. Before the Longships lighthouse was built, these rocks caused a navigational nightmare for mariners attempting to round the headland safely, especially at night. A few miles away the Wolf Rock (SW 268120) and Runnel Stone (SW 369201) outcrops added to the problems, and the number of shipping disasters and drownings since time immemorial hardly bear thinking about.

A map of 1702 marks a proposed lighthouse on the cliff at Pordenack Point, just south of Land's End, and there are archaeological remains of a structure here which may have been a Napoleonic signal station marked on a map of 1809.

The main group of rocks off Land's End is the Longships (latitude and longitude 50° 4' 1" N., 5° 44' 49" W), with its three larger outcrops: Meinek (SW 321254), Carn Brâs or Carnvroaz (SW 320253)

A turbulent mass of currents and tides.
Peter Puddiphatt

3

The Longships lighthouse alerts mariners to the dangerous rocks in its vicinity. *Courtesy Trinity House*

and Tal-y-Maen (SW 323250). Other well-known ones are Kettle's Bottom and Shark's Fin. A demand for some kind of sea mark in this area had been mooted for a very long time and, in the 1780s, one man's vision to provide safe passage for all mariners was born. By 1795 the first Longships lighthouse was established on Carn Brâs and was the saviour of countless seafarers, and its Trinity House replacement, completed in 1873-4, remains a main attraction seen from the cliffs at Land's End.

In 1514, Henry VIII issued a Royal Charter enabling a group of mariners, known as the Guild of the Holy Trinity, to regulate the pilotage of ships. Elder Brethren comprised a Master, Wardens and Assistants, while the Younger Brethren formed the majority. They became known as the Corporation of Trinity House, and their headquarters were at Deptford on the River Thames. In 1836 Trinity House was given the power to compulsorily purchase all private lighthouses and to maintain and manage them. Today, they maintain 69 lighthouses, both on isolated rocks and on the mainland.

CHAPTER ONE

The first lighthouse

A keen interest in providing the means of safer navigation around Land's End was taken by Lieutenant Henry Smith, RN in the 1780s. In 1781-2 he had sailed around the south-west coast in *HMS Squirrel* on his first commission. As early as March 1782 he had travelled from Penzance to London to visit Trinity House and shown them a model he had made of a lighthouse upon the Longships reef.

Nothing happened for the next few years, but Smith retained his interest in a lighthouse and also in sea marks for the Runnel Stone and Wolf Rock, both notorious wreckers of ships. In September 1790, he sent Trinity House numerous requests from 'Merchants, Owners and Masters of Ships' for lights and marks. John Smeaton went out to survey the Longships reef but was not convinced of its suitability for a lighthouse and was unable to give an indication of probable costs.

In April 1791 Smith recommended to the Corporation a lighthouse on the Longships and the placing of sea marks made of oak trees or other 'substantial & conspicuous' materials on the Runnel Stone and Wolf Rock. In May he received a lease for a period of 50 years from when the first lights were to be exhibited, at a rent of £100 p.a. The Patent was granted on 30 June 1791.

Once preparatory work had started on the Longships in 1791 Smith encountered opposition to the lighthouse from local inhabitants in and around the Land's End peninsula. Eventually, at the end of July, he wrote to Trinity House requesting protection for seven

Directions for ships sailing by the Longships lighthouse 1795. *Courtesy Trinity House*

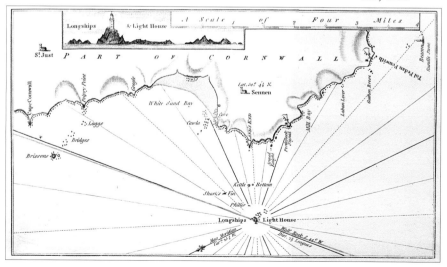

Trinity House plan of the 1795 light-house.
Courtesy Association of Lighthouse Keepers

men in the sloop *Happy Return* when carrying stores and materials out to the Longships. The Elder Brethren ordered that a Certificate be made out for them under the Seal of the Corporation.

A Devon newspaper reported that on Sunday 18 September 1791, 'Mr Smith, accompanied by more of the gentlemen of this town [Penzance] and neighbourhood, proceeded to the Land's End, to lay the first stone of a new Light-House, that is to be built on the Long Ships.'

The architect of the Longships lighthouse is thought to have been Samuel Wyatt, Surveyor for Trinity House. Stone for the building was local granite, and it is presumed that these stones were dressed and fitted together by trenailing and dovetailing at a base in Sennen Cove before being shipped out to Carn Brâs.

By the summer of 1793 the lantern of the lighthouse with the gallery was completed, and the railing was being fixed.

In April 1795 Wyatt, accompanied by Elder Brethren Capt Joseph Huddart, went out to survey the lighthouse. Wyatt found it substantially built and well executed to answer the purpose, 'but in order to render it of general use to the Trade as was intended, it will be necessary to extend the light of it to the Northwest and Southward, by glazing the Lanthorn ¾ round instead of $5/16$ as at present, and by increasing the Number of Reflectors and Lamps to Eighteen instead of Eight as now fixed.'

As Smith was now in the Kings Bench Prison for debtors (see below), he had difficulties organising the work and, in the end, Capt Huddart had to intervene, drawing up plans for the sea marks, which were then successfully erected, and overseeing the finishing touches to the lighthouse.

Finally, on 18 September 1795, Capt Huddart announced that alterations to the lantern and lamps had been made satisfactorily and that the poles had been fixed permanently. The order was made to exhibit the light and to keep it constantly burning from sunset to sunrise. Tolls and dues were to be collected from then onwards.

And so, at long last, on Tuesday 29 September 1795, the first exhibition of light took place on the Longships lighthouse. It had been constructed at a cost of £41,188 10s 1d.

Built on rock about 38 feet above high tide, the circular lighthouse comprised Cornish granite stones dovetailed into each other and into the bed rock, secured by oak trenails and strong cement - a technique developed for Smeaton's Eddystone lighthouse. It stood three storeys high, plus the lantern room, on a roughly square granite platform.

The structure had 25 courses of stone from the top of the base to under the lantern; the walls were four feet thick at the base tapering to three feet six inches at the first floor and to three feet at the second floor. Three windows graced the south elevation, two on both the west and east and two on the north, above the door.

A survey of the lighthouse in 1828. *Courtesy Trinity House*

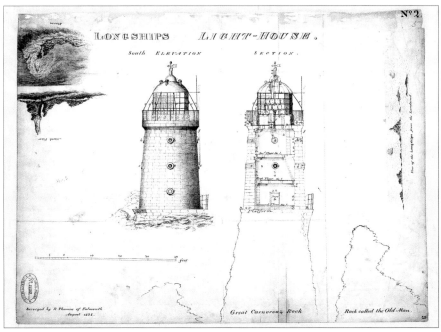

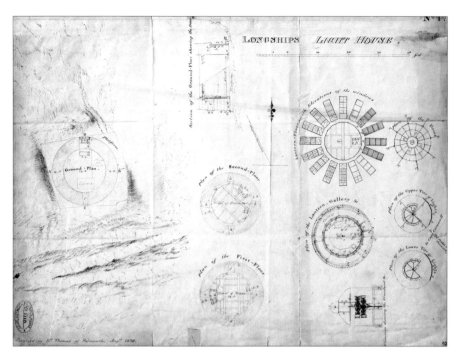

Floor plans of the lighthouse in 1828. *Courtesy Trinity House*

The height from its base to the arrow-shaped weather vane was 52 feet and the height of the lantern above the high water spring tide was 79 feet. The distance of the sea horizon from the light was 9½ miles and, in clear weather, from 18 feet above the water the light could be seen 14 miles away with the naked eye.

Internally, plans reveal that the diameter of the ground floor measured 14 feet one inch, it had a height of six feet nine inches and a door three feet six inches wide; it also had a raised floor. To the left of the door was storage for coals, while against the south wall was a cistern for fresh water which, according to Robert Stevenson visiting in 1818, was made of wood.

An oak ladder and trap door to the right of the door led to the first floor, the diameter of which was 14 feet one inch. It was seven feet high and four feet one inch from floor to window; the window openings were two feet five inches wide internally, tapering to 11 inches externally. In this room was the kitchen and oil store.

Another oak ladder led to the second floor with a diameter of 14 feet one inch, and height of seven feet eight inches; the window openings were two feet wide internally, tapering to nine inches externally. This doubled up as both the living room and bedroom.

The octagonal lantern room which housed the lighting equipment was reached by another oak ladder. The glazed section of the lantern, which was seven feet four inches high, comprised 16 vertical windows, 12 of which were divided into four panes of glass, some of which were sub-divided into smaller panes. The other four panes were blanked out in metal to protect the land from the bright light. The frames were made from oak and copper. The diameter of the lantern room was 11 feet nine inches, and around three quarters of its perimeter was a platform one foot eight inches in width. The metalwork was copper. There was also a stove in the lantern room.

Plans show 19 burners were arranged in two tiers with nine on the lower one and ten on the upper one, and with a range from Tol-Pedn-Penwith to Cape Cornwall, a distance of about 7½km (just under 5 miles) distance. The light itself was fixed rather than revolving, and comprised a catoptric apparatus (rays from a light source being reflected by mirrors) with Argand lamps, and parabolic reflectors 21 inches in diameter and nine inches deep, and gave a bright light. The reflectors and frame were made by George Robinson, London, and the lamps were made by R. Wilkins & Son, London. Dr Michael Faraday's ventilating apparatus cost £59 19s 6d.

A domed roof capped the lantern room on top of which were fixed a funnel and cowl. A weather vane with an arrow crowned the entire lighthouse. A door led from the lantern room to the gallery which was two feet one inch wide, and a parapet whose low wall, one foot five inches wide, had two courses of granite two feet two inches in height into which narrowly-spaced iron railings were fixed giving an additional height of three feet six inches. Metal stays were attached from the dome to the gallery. There was also a flag staff and a lightning conductor to Dr Faraday's design.

Four lighthouse keepers from St Just, on a salary of £30 p.a.,

Views of the
Longships
lighthouse by
H. B. Bax.
*Courtesy Association
of Lighthouse
Keepers*

9

Priest's Cove, known as Porth St Just.
Elisabeth Stanbrook Collection

were employed to man the lighthouse, two at a time working for one month, and then a changeover effected by a relief boat and crew, weather permitting. This relief boat was kept at Porth St Just, Cape Cornwall, now known as Priest's Cove, where there was a capstan and a store which had been built 'partially underground.' The first Agent, Mr John Dunkin, was employed to oversee the smooth running of the reliefs and all the supplies needed for the lighthouse.

View from Priest's Cove's modernised slipway towards the lighthouse.
Elisabeth Stanbrook

Financial problems

Smith had overstretched himself financially, borrowing money and not managing it well. His creditors began to demand the return of their loans, and early 1795 saw him a prisoner in the Kings Bench Prison. Trinity House became extremely concerned about 'his improvident heedless conduct', and about any liabilities that might arise which Smith would be unable to pay, so they demanded a bond of £10,000 in return for granting him the lease for the tolls.

The problems rumbled on with Smith desperately trying to solve his dire predicament from prison and attempting to raise a mortgage to pay off his creditors. On 13 December 1796 he was committed to Fleet Prison and, by July 1797 he was, unsurprisingly, causing the light to be neglected and the reserves of oil to run very low. Trinity House filed a Bill to obtain leave of the Court of Chancery 'to have the direction of the supply of oil and all other necessities and sufficient light keepers lest the public should suffer any failure in exhibition of light.' Any profits from the tolls would be paid to Smith's family through the Court of Chancery.

The application was granted and, on 22 June 1798, Trinity House took charge of the lighthouse, conducted an inspection and left it in the care of four people, after which they appointed Mr John Millett of St Just as Agent with a salary of £30 p.a.

Deposed Agent, Mr Dunkin, was probably not pleased at suddenly losing his post and salary, and the Corporation was compelled to issue him with a warning 'at his peril to try and desist from molesting the persons appointed to the care of the light or interfering in any way.'

Under new management the lighthouse's condition and efficiency improved vastly, and by October Mr Millett was able to report that all was in good repair 'and the Light much brighter since the dead Lights were taken out.' Supplies were being forwarded to the lighthouse by relief boatman Mr Richard Jewel Ferris, who was to receive a gratuity of £10 p.a. for this service.

An engraving from 1842 by G. F. Sargeant.

CHAPTER TWO

The early nineteenth century

In 1801 lighthouse engineer, Robert Stevenson visited the Longships. 'Having had on three different nights an opportunity to see this light, I was much pleased with the brilliant effect of its reflectors and I do not think it necessary to exhibit a much stronger light than this.' But he was less impressed with the keepers baking their meat in the lantern.

Stevenson interviewed Smith in Fleet Prison in 1806 about difficulties that had arisen over the building of the lighthouse. He concluded that Smith 'had no real capacity for sea-works.' Smith died intestate on 28 October 1809, leaving a widow and four children.

In January 1815 a terrific gale blew in, whipping up the sea into a frenzy of frothing foam, obscuring the lighthouse from the land. Local and national newspapers reported that the Longships lighthouse had been completely destroyed and that all vessels should beware. However, these reports were false. A letter from the Agent, Mr Millett of 7 January said 'the sea made a common Break over the Light House, by which means many of the Panes in the Lanthorn were broke, which prevented the Light Keepers from shewing so good a Light as usual.' The damage was repaired and the light made as good as ever.

In 1818 Robert Stevenson visited the Longships lighthouse again and found the place to be in a very bad state. Initially the 'very ragged and wild-like' keepers refused him permission to enter and it crossed his mind that they may have wanted to either extract money or prevent him seeing the state of the place which 'was in the worst

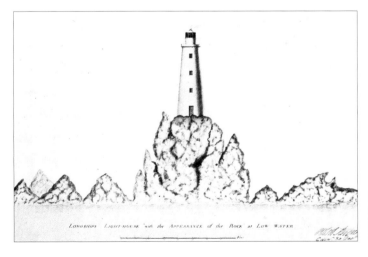

Robert Stevenson's engraving of the Longships lighthouse in 1801

13

VIEW of the LAND'S END, and LONGSHIP'S LIGHT-HOUSE, FROM THE SEA,
DRAWN BY LIEUTENANT PARKER, R. N.

An engraving of the lighthouse in 1820, by Lieut Parker.

possible order.' But having gained entry, the keepers did not show any shame at the state of the lighthouse. 'What an effluvia of fish met us on entering the house! In the kitchen the fireplace was unfit for a fire and all the meat is baked in the lantern – it was the same in 1801. The reflectors were quite dim and everything was dirty – of course I found the light at 2 this morning quite red-coloured. ...No person to inspect has been here for four years.'

In a letter dated 22 November 1824 Mr James Trembath of Mayon House, Sennen wrote saying that a signal (flag) had been hoisted on the lighthouse on and off for three weeks. On Saturday 20 November Mr Steen, Second Setter of the boat belonging to the Preventative Service, went with some of his men to the lighthouse and found that the keepers were in want of meat, sugar, tea and water etc. The Agent at St Just (who was now Mr Nicholas Boyns) was told of their plight. Mr Trembath felt this proved that Sennen Cove was superior to Porth St Just as a situation for the Longships boats, and that the Agent was inattentive and inefficient. Trinity House ordered provisions to be sent to the lighthouse immediately, and asked Boyns to explain himself. His reply was not recorded, but somehow he escaped dismissal.

In 1825 two keepers, Bottrell and White, were admitting numerous people to the lighthouse who were smuggling in alcohol on which they were becoming intoxicated. As a result, Trinity House dismissed White and appointed John Clements in his place. Clements was to become the subject of one of the Longships oft-told tales (see below).

Meanwhile, there were still issues arising from Lieut Smith's mismanagement. Henry Pascoe Smith was the representative lessee and had to contend with claims made against his father's estate by disgruntled parties. For example, in May 1824 Mr Alexander Woolcock made a claim for £97 for work on building the lighthouse; in April 1828 there was an inquiry in respect of wages said to be due to a labourer employed in erecting the lighthouse, and in February 1833 there was a claim for £42 due to the surviving children of another lighthouse builder, Joseph Phillips.

Trinity House acquires the lighthouse

A Trinity House examination of the lighthouse and rock took place on 12 August 1830. It was reported that the tower 'remains perfect.' East of the lighthouse they commented on the high part of the rock detached from that on which it stood, forming a chasm from one to four yards in width. It had been suggested to fill it up 'with mason's work' but it was felt the chasm through which the sea broke with much violence in northerly gales had not undergone any alteration for many years and, if filled up, would be expensive and 'might be productive of mischief' if not made as secure as the rock.

For 1831 and 1832 the gross collection of lighthouse duties received for the Longships was £7,393; after various expenses and taxes, the net profit to Henry Pascoe Smith (Lieut Henry Smith's son) was £5,036. By 1836 it had risen to £8,293. These profits had risen considerably each year, and Mr Hume MP was highly critical of Trinity House and their allowing private individuals to build lighthouses and receive income, describing it as 'a system of jobbing and plunder.'

Wild weather at the Longships. *Courtesy Association of Lighthouse Keepers*

Artist J. M. W. Turner's view of the Longships lighthouse (left). From an old print. *Elisabeth Stanbrook Collection*

This scathing attack prompted the Corporation to negotiate with the Smith family for the Longships lighthouse lease and duties.

Negotiations went on until March 1836 when both parties reached an agreement for Trinity House to purchase the remaining nine and a half years left on the lease for £37,475 9s 2d (£40,676 including the purchase of annuities).

While these negotiations were taking place, an Act of Parliament (passed on 13 August 1836) was being drafted, empowering the Corporation to compulsorily purchase all lighthouses, lights and sea marks around the English coast. A standard light due was to be introduced for all vessels, and the income would be used for lighthouse building and maintenance.

Agent, keepers and boatmen

The Agent's and keepers' pay of £30 p.a. had remained unaltered for years. In July 1836 keepers John Grills, John Clements, William Thomas and Richard Trehair, successfully petitioned Trinity House to allow them and the Agent to have an extra 10s per month.

In April 1838 an inspection by the Corporation found the lighthouse in a dirty and unsatisfactory condition. It was ordered that the keepers 'be severely reprimanded for their inattention in that respect and at the same time apprized that if Habits of strict Cleanliness are not on the next Inspection found to exist thereat the Board will immediately dismiss them from their situations.'

Agent Nicholas Boyns wrote to Trinity House regarding a huge

storm on 29 November 1838, 'the Sea ran so very tremendous as to break in one of the panes of the Glass and to strike out 16 of the Lamps leaving only 3 lighted, at which time a great Quantity of Water went down through the House'.

This may be the storm which gave rise to the story about the keeper whose hair turned white while on duty. A newspaper of 1842 recounts the tale of John Clements who, a few years previously, witnessed a terrific hurricane while on duty in the lighthouse; 'the wind was so strong and the sea so high, that Clements and his companion could not be relieved for a period of 15 weeks. But when they were relieved, and had reached the shore, our readers may judge of the astonishment of Clements' relatives and friends when they discovered that he who, a short time before, had left them with very dark hair, had now returned with hair quite white! And not only so, but that his eye-brows and eye-lashes were also changed to the same colour!!' The report came from someone who knew Clements, so it suggests an element of truth in the tale.

In 1842 Boyns informed Trinity House that Mark Williams had died. He had been a boat crewman for nearly 20 years (and also worked as a tin miner). His widow was too poor to pay for his funeral so Boyns had given her 30s and asked for reimbursement, which he was given. It may have been Williams's son George who, in 1854, was dismissed as boatman by Mr Boyns. It was also in 1854 that Nicholas Boyns retired from his post as Agent after 32 years' service, receiving a pension of £25. His son became his successor.

From Land's End in 1840, by S. Owen. *Elisabeth Stanbrook Collection*

From a sketch by R. T. Pentreath c.1845

CHAPTER THREE

The move to Sennen

The 1850s saw major changes in the local administration of the Longships lighthouse. Mr James Trembath wrote to Trinity House in November 1854 repeating his view that, 'Sennen Cove would undoubtedly be the best station for the Boats' and that he would accommodate them and the stores on his land at Sennen. Everything was still being undertaken from St Just, where 'the lightkeepers lodge … and the store at that place is largely underground and is held under an agreement with Mr John Batten at a rent of £5 p.a.'

Trembath also recommended that Matthew Nicholas, coxswain of the Sennen lifeboat, would be ideal to take charge of the lighthouse boat and stores.

Trinity House was in agreement with Trembath's sentiments, also deciding that to house the keepers at Sennen would be prudent. So in May 1855 they invited tenders for erecting four dwellings, a store and a boat house at Sennen on land to be bought from Mr Trembath. The work was given to Mr Harvey in May 1856, who undertook all the building work for £960.

The four dwellings were built on a triangular piece of land to the east of Mayon Cliff at SW 353258 and, although no longer in Trinity

James Trembath.
Courtesy
Tony Millett

Mayon House, home of James Trembath.
Elisabeth Stanbrook

Trinity House dwellings built in the 1850s for the lighthouse keepers. *Elisabeth Stanbrook*

House ownership, survive today as a distinctive row of properties. They were built of stone with stone floors and a slate roof. Upstairs were the bedrooms while downstairs each had a sitting room, kitchen and 'back kitchen'. Outside, each had a coal house, privy and piggery.

Trinity House emblem above the store window and door. *Elisabeth Stanbrook*

The Store was in the Cove and still bears the Corporation emblem above the front door. It was built at the west end of the Cove above the car park at SW 350263. It was a substantial single-storey property of stone and slate measuring approximately 44 feet long, 18 feet wide and 18 feet tall.

In March 1856 the keepers' water supply ran so low that an unscheduled delivery of this and other supplies had to be made. Unfortunately, Matthew Nicholas and his Longships boat crew were overtaken by a violent storm en route to the lighthouse, and the Sennen lifeboat had to go to their assistance. Trinity House, who had seemed unaware of the keepers' plight, awarded the relief boat crew £10 compensation for their exertions, and was to reprimand Mr Boyns if he proved responsible for the low supplies. Two years later Mr Boyns was replaced as Agent for the Longships (and Godrevy) by Mr J. N. Tremearne of St Ives, Cornwall.

In 1857 another storm caused problems for the keepers when, on 7 October, seven of the 19 lamps were extinguished for one hour by the sea penetrating between the lower part of the cowl and the 'petticoat'.

The former Trinity House store built in c.1856. *Elisabeth Stanbrook*

CHAPTER FOUR

Trinity House inspection of 1859

A Royal Commission Report of 1861 reveals that a Trinity House inspection party visited the Longships in their vessel *Vivid* in July 1859 and found all in good order. The light and catoptric reflectors were bright and well polished, the house was being painted and was also in good order, and the log was properly kept by the keepers. Since its purchase, from 1836 to 1858, the average annual costs of repairs had been £36 3s 7d, while the cost of painting it every four years had been £21 19s 9d.

The Report mentioned the loud sound from the cavern under the lighthouse; '... when there is a heavy sea the noise produced from the escape of pent-up air from the cavern is so great that the men can hardly sleep. It was stated that one man was so terrified that his hair turned white' – a reference to keeper John Clements.

The lighthouse had always had just two keepers on duty at any one time, but the Report revealed that, 'We have just succeeded in

One of the earliest known photographs, taken by C. R. Lobb in 1866.
Elisabeth Stanbrook Collection

Three keepers pose for a photograph by C. R. Lobb in 1866. *Courtesy Association of Lighthouse Keepers*

getting permission from the Board of Trade to have a third man always present at a rock station.' This is interesting because one of the tales attached to the Longships lighthouse is that of a keeper dying on duty at the lighthouse, leaving the remaining keeper with the body. He had to fulfil all duties on his own until help could arrive, and that this had prompted the installation of three keepers. On 3 April 1855, Keeper William Thomas died on Longships lighthouse age 65, so this incident was likely to have been that responsible for the change in the way all rock stations were manned. A similar event occurred on the Smalls lighthouse off the Welsh coast in 1801.

The Principal Keeper's (PK) salary was £60 p.a. and the three Assistant Keepers (AK) were now receiving £49 10s p.a. with an allowance of 1s 6d per day per man for victualling, a suit of clothes annually and coal, oil and furniture for the living rooms. The relief was once a month. Three of the four keepers were now always at the lighthouse with one on shore in rotation. They were relieved by the hired sailing boat owned by Matthew Nicholas.

The head keeper had previously been at the Eddystone lighthouse and told the visiting committee he preferred that station although the sea was just as bad there. On the Longships he described heavy weather in which waves broke about the lantern

79 feet above the high-water mark. 'On one occasion the sea lifted the cowl off the top so as to admit a great deal of water. Several lamps were extinguished, and all the men were employed in baling out water till the tide fell.' He was probably referring to the storm of 1857.

Tragedies at the lighthouse

Another fatality occurred at the Longships which bore out the need for three keepers. On 27 September 1861 Assistant Keeper Frederick Samuel Howard, age 37, committed suicide by stabbing himself in the stomach with his clasp knife. At the inquest held the following Friday Matthew Nicholas, the relief boatman, told how, at 10am, he had seen a signal (probably black flags) from the lighthouse indicating that medical assistance was required. He gathered a crew of men and set out for the lighthouse where he was taken to the sleeping quarters. Howard was lying on his mattress in a 'dying state', and Matthew Nicholas was shown a long clasp spring knife covered in blood by Principal Keeper Cock. Howard was got into the boat as quickly as possible and taken to the mainland for medical attention, but to no avail. A verdict was given of death by a self-inflicted stab wound while labouring under temporary insanity.

There were two more fatalities at the Longships in 1866-7 when keepers Mr Bell and Mr Henderson disappeared, swept from the rock while outside.

There are several early paintings and etchings of the Longships lighthouse, but some of the earliest photographs were taken in 1866 by Mr C. R. Lobb, a Wadebridge photographer. It is likely that Trinity House commissioned him to take them and, in September of that year, the 'account of Mr Lobb for photographs of the Longships, recently supplied by him, amounting to £2 2s' was paid.

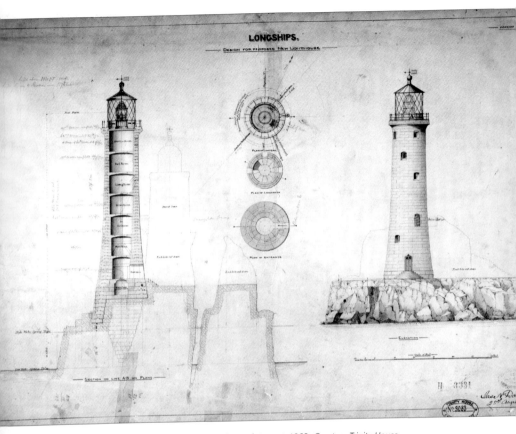

The new lighthouse plans of August 1868. *Courtesy Trinity House*

24

CHAPTER FIVE

Plans for a new lighthouse

By 1868, the question of a new lighthouse on the Longships had been decided. The constantly crashing waves over the lantern during storms gave the light the appearance of an occulting light rather than fixed, which caused some confusion for mariners. The light could be completely obscured by the force of the sea spray. Huge waves coming in from the Atlantic would hit the structure, travel onwards to Land's End only to be bounced off the cliffs and back to the lighthouse. Occasionally one of these returning waves would clash with a new wave. The condition of the rock on which the Wyatt structure stood was becoming unsafe due to the natural chasm becoming unstable.

Some authors claim it was William Douglass, brother of Trinity House Engineer Sir James, who surveyed and designed the new lighthouse. The biographer of Sir James Douglass, who had served under him for 30 years, and which would have included this period, says quite plainly that it was James who designed the lighthouse, and contemporary documents bear this out.

Having surveyed the rock James Douglass recommended a tower of granite upon a base adjoining that of the Wyatt lighthouse. It would carry a first order fixed dioptric light (using lenses and prisms to refract the light) at 110 ft above high water spring tides. The estimated cost was £41,200 which the Board of Trade sanctioned on 30 September 1868, together with a temporary light while the works were being carried out.

The workmen employed on the lighthouse would need to embark from Sennen Cove. Somewhere for them to lodge became a necessity and, at the end of 1869, Mr John Symons, brother-in-law of Mr James Trembath, offered land on which to build a barracks with a storeyard as well as a slipway for use by the workmen.

The wooden barracks were built on the sea front and, after Trinity House had finished with the building, local clergyman Rev Roe acquired it to use as a Mission Room in which to hold

James Douglass.
Courtesy Institution of Civil Engineers

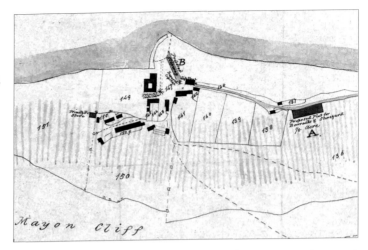

Plans drawn up in 1870 for the barracks and new slipway, coloured red. The existing store is also in red, on the left.
Courtesy Trinity House

weekly meetings. It was also used as a Reading Room, and was put up for sale in the auction of Sennen properties in 1922, with a condition that the building would be removed and the site ready by Christmas. There is no indication that it sold, but it was eventually demolished and another building sits in its place.

The workmen were to receive 'rock-money' - an additional 4d per hour when working on the rock, or 2d per hour if lodged on the rock.

After careful consideration, it was decided to ask Mr Hardingham's Lamorna Granite Company to provide scappled stone (dressed with the pick end of a hammer) for the tower at 1s 11d per

The former barracks became a Mission Hall and a Reading Room.
Angove Collection

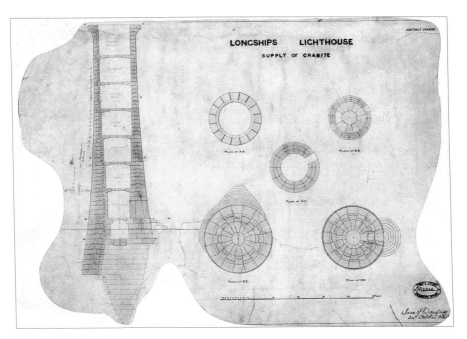

LONGSHIPS LIGHTHOUSE

SUPPLY OF GRANITE

PLAN AT A.A.

PLAN AT B.B.

PLAN AT C.C.

PLAN AT E.E.

PLAN AT D.D.

cubic foot and small ashlar for the landing places at 1s 9d per cubic foot. Mr J. Thorel of Dinan Quarry, Morlaix, France, was to be asked to provide the dressed off-set courses, steps, landings and coping for landing places at 3s 8d per cubic foot.

A 'Contract Drawing' for the supply of granite, dated October 1868. *Courtesy Trinity House*

Many of the masons and workmen, and the vessels and plant used for the just-completed Wolf Rock lighthouse were now to be employed on the Longships.

In late February 1869, once contracts had been finalised with

Lamorna Quarry. *Illustrated London News.*

Lamorna Cove and Quarry from an old postcard.
Elisabeth Stanbrook Collection

Dinan Quarries and Lamorna Granite Company, James Douglass was instructed to proceed with the construction of the new lighthouse. Mr Michael Beazeley, who had replaced William Douglass as Resident Engineer on the Wolf Rock, was now appointed to oversee the building of the new lighthouse.

Problems with building and supplies

That some of the stone was to be imported from France did not go down too well with the Cornish and caused comment about lost revenue and wages in local newspapers:

> From perfidius Gaul, hewn and shaped from the hands of men whose fathers, 60 years ago, cut English throats, will come the stalwart blocks, the topmost of which must bear a friendly light… English men might have had the job and gained the advantageous circulation of many thousands of wages among their neighbours…

On 5 August 1869 a silver penny from the reign of King Edward I (1272 – 1307) was found by the Principal Keeper of the Longships in a crevice of a rock where workmen were preparing for the new tower. The coin was placed in Trinity House Museum in London.

The building work and supply of granite did not go smoothly, the contractors causing delays and problems. In August 1869 James Douglass made an inspection of the Dinan Quarries and commented on the unsatisfactory supply of stone.

In the meantime, Lamorna Granite Company was causing problems. In October 1869 they had provided some inferior granite. In December the Engineer went to inspect Lamorna Quarry for himself and concluded that a sufficient quantity of stone could not be relied upon without assistance from a neighbouring quarry belonging to Messrs Freeman & Sons who then supplied 280 cubic feet each week.

Lamorna Granite Company continued to have difficulties and, in 1870, the order for the scappled stone got into arrears. So again, Messrs Freeman offered to supply 6,000 cubic feet of scappled stone at 2s 6d per cubic foot.

That February another lighthouse keeper, Mr Smith aged 50 years, drowned when he slipped or was swept off the rock by a wave while throwing ashes into the sea. The keepers hoisted a distress flag, but due to dense fog it was not seen until the following day. The rough weather meant a landing could not be effected on the rock for a few days.

The building of the new lighthouse continued apace, the stone being prepared at Trinity House's Penzance workyard.

A new landing place, started in 1870, was built by summer 1871 at the north point of the rock. From here a powerful crane and winch were fixed for discharging stone from barges and landing it on a tramway connected with the tower from where it was lifted into position by a crane fixed in the centre of the work. Two other landing places were also built – the south landing and the Pollard or Bridges to the east with planks of iron or granite spanning three small islets.

Problems still continued with supplies of stone from both sides of the English Channel, and in September 1871, James Douglass had to send Trinity House a telegram saying that the tug *Solva* had caught

Plan of the rock and landing places. *Courtesy Trinity House*

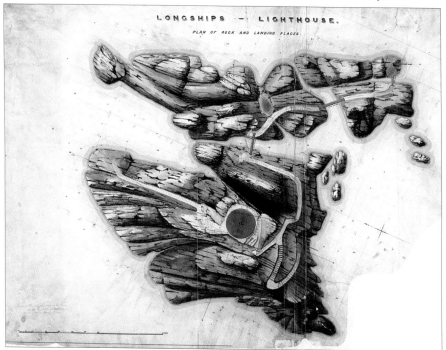

LONGSHIPS — LIGHTHOUSE.

PLAN OF ROCK AND LANDING PLACES.

fire. It had been extinguished fairly quickly, but Mr Beazeley was reprimanded for the want of a proper watch and supervision which might have prevented the accident.

The contract for the gun metal doors for lighthouse was awarded to Messrs Deville & Co.

Despite all the various problems, 1 August 1871 had been a day of celebration when the foundation stone for the new lighthouse was laid. The steam tug *Solva* and a barge with the workmen went out to Longships with Resident Engineer Mr Beazeley, who laid the two-ton foundation stone of French granite at around noon. It was 'lowered into position amidst loud cheering.' Rev R. Roe, vicar of Sennen, then offered prayers and blessed the work to come. This was met with three cheers.

Messrs Turner & Co were awarded the contract for the lantern in early 1872, which was completed in August. Messrs Chance Brothers provided the first order dioptric apparatus at £2,140. The apparatus was powered by a spring operated drive which had to be wound up every six hours. The light itself was an eight-wick Douglass lamp.

The metal fog bell for the Longships, ordered by the Corporation from Messrs Mears & Co, would sound 'a quick double stroke every quarter minute.'

In August 1872 Land's End area residents and visitors saw flags suspended on poles and a large number of people on the upper storey of the Longships lighthouse below the lantern, and the distant sound of cheering. A local Freemason, probably Sir Frederick Arrow, Knt., had laid the capstone of the lighthouse, a momentous occasion. Mr Beazeley hoped to have the new and stronger light operational by New Year's Day. 'To celebrate the completion of the masonry Mrs Beazeley gave 63 of the workmen, etc, a capital supper… at Penzance.' Above the entrance door to the lighthouse a stone dated 1872 was placed.

Yet another lighthouse keeper lost his life at the Longships on 5 December 1872. John Palmer had gone down to the landing place to pull in a fishing net when a sudden wave carried him off. The other keepers threw him a lifebuoy and rope but he could not grasp them. William Thomas, a carpenter at the Longships works, risked his own life to try and save him, and a silver watch to a value of £5 was presented to him with an inscription engraved upon it 'in token of admiration of his praiseworthy conduct'. He was also awarded the bronze medal and clasp of the Royal Humane Society for attempting to save his life.

Christmas 1872 saw 15 workmen marooned on the Longships and provisions ran very low. They signalled for supplies on Christmas Eve, but bad weather prevented any relief boat attending until 30 December. The lighthouse keepers shared their own provisions with the workmen.

An old postcard showing the white painted wall surrounding the entrance door for semaphore purposes. *Elisabeth Stanbrook Collection*

The lighthouse is finished

On 5 December 1873 the new first order dioptric light was exhibited for the first time. The illuminating apparatus itself showed a fixed white light with red sectors illuminating the adjacent dangers of the Runnel Stone and Brisons rocks off Cape Cornwall.

The building of the new Longships lighthouse cost £43,869 8s 11d and comprised 47,610 cubic feet of granite.

The new lighthouse had 65 courses of granite, at least eight of them below the high water spring tide level. Granite steps led up to the gun metal entrance door, and the windows were also constructed of gun metal. Below this entrance level was the water storage room, while the floor above was the coal store. Above that was the oil room with an external door for receiving deliveries which would be hauled up in barrels, and on top of that was a store room which doubled up as a kitchen. Domestic rooms came next; the living room and then the bedroom with its banana-shaped beds about five feet nine inches at the longest point, followed by the service room. The fittings and fixtures for each room had to be specially designed to accommodate the circular walls. Each floor was linked by an iron staircase. Crowning all the floors were the lantern and gallery, topped with a ball finial ventilator, a lightning conductor and a weather vane.

Outside the entrance door the surrounding wall was painted white so that the keepers could communicate to the shore by semaphore.

The new tower still vibrated in violent weather, but the foundations were safely embedded into the bedrock. Near the lighthouse was the large chasm in the rock in which was a huge boulder. A lighthouse keeper recalled that about 36 hours before a big sea arrived, a ground swell would form, moving the boulder around in the chasm. Thus they were forewarned of an impending storm.

In February 1874 Trinity House employed Mr Dixon as Clerk of Works under Michael Beazeley, at five guineas a week. He had to oversee the finishing of fine details such as the fixing of mooring chains, and the dismantling of the Wyatt lighthouse. The tender of Mr Richards for the supply of a new wooden boat for service of Longships for £22 15s was accepted, and one dozen maroon rockets of the corporate pattern in a copper case were to be installed.

The *Royal Cornwall Gazette* reported that a tremendous gale on 13 April 1874 had dislodged 'a huge piece of rock, scores of tons in weight' on Carn Brâs, the site of the old lighthouse. The whole rock was moved *en masse* about a foot.'

The drowning of PK Smith from the Longships occurred on 12 February 1875, and a warning notice was issued to keepers on Rock Stations.

The novel *The Watchers on the Longships* was published in 1878. Written by author James F. Cobb, it concerned the kidnapping of a lighthouse keeper by Cornish wreckers to prevent the light from being lit and therefore encouraging ships to founder on the rocks. The keeper's daughter, who was living there, managed to keep the light lit by standing on a bible to reach the candles. There is no documentary evidence to authenticate this tale, but it has become part of the folklore of the lighthouse.

It was only a year later that one of the youngest lighthouse keepers lost his life while on duty. On 25 October 1877 18 year-old Owen Boyle was swept off the rock and it was not until November that his body was found by the lifeboat crew under the cliffs of St Just. A memorial window was installed in St Just church in 1879 by his parents. It reads: 'In affectionate remembrance of Owen Boyle, lightkeeper, the only beloved son of Owen & Margaret Boyle, who lost his life at the Longships lighthouse, 25th October 1877, aged 18 years & 6 months. May he rest in peace Amen.'

The window in St Just's church dedicated to Keeper Owen Boyle.
Elisabeth Stanbrook

In the late summer of 1878 members of the Elder Brethren inspected the Longships lighthouse. Afterwards they ascended the church tower at Sennen to make a trigonometrical estimate of the exact height of the lighthouse. It must have met with their approval as no remedial work was recommended.

In 1882 the light at the Longships was altered to one occultation or flash per minute.

Sennen church from where a trigonometrical estimate of the exact height of the lighthouse was made.
Elisabeth Stanbrook

The 1882 plan for the intermittent or occulting light. *Courtesy Trinity House*

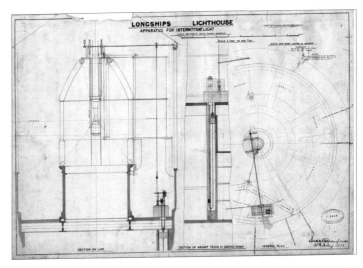

Plan of 1883 of the apparatus for firing gun cotton charges. *Courtesy Trinity House*

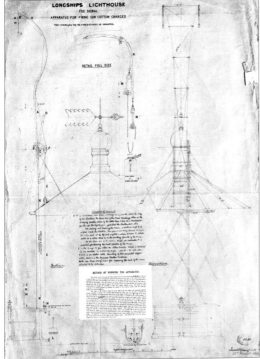

That same year Sir James Douglass's method of fog signalling with gun cotton charges was tried at the Longships from the lantern gallery. The result, recorded on 13 September, was considered very satisfactory and discussions on their use at the lighthouse continued with a design drawn up by the Engineer in March 1883. That it was installed is evident from a local newspaper report which stated 'that the fog signal on the Longships can be heard in Penzance and [the charges] are of gun cotton. Half a pound of gun cotton makes as loud a report as 3lbs gunpowder.' There were two charges every ten minutes.

CHAPTER SIX

Alterations and repairs

During 1892 the light was converted to burning heavy mineral oil. New oil cisterns were installed at a cost of £88. Three additional 140 gallon oil cisterns were put in place in 1897 at a cost of £47 5s.

A new explosive fog signal apparatus was installed during this time. In November 1890 two new exploders were obtained from the Cotton Powder Company at a cost of £8 8s 6d, and protective apparatus supplied. A third exploder was added in 1893 as a standby to be suspended from the firing jib of the explosive signals. In 1898 there was an alteration in the character of the explosive fog signal from two reports every ten minutes to two reports every five minutes, at an annual cost of £152.

The three landing places constructed for the lighthouse also needed constant attention as wave action and storm damage were relentless; for example, in December 1891 a storm swept away one landing place and a relief could not be made from another for a fortnight. On relief days, when the sea was too rough to be able to step ashore, the keepers were landed by breeches buoy, the situation reversed for returning men. Supplies were also landed by ropes.

In 1892 the Light Committee decided upon a new semaphore at the Longships and arrangements were made with the Admiralty for Longships and Trevose Head to use their telegraph wires for their occasional use; in 1895 £10 was spent on new flashing signal lamps and, in 1896, new pressure lamps were supplied.

Supplies being landed from a boat c. 1892.
Elisabeth Stanbrook Collection

One of the bridges which suffered constant damage.
J. Harris Stone

A drawing of Matthew Nicholas which appeared in *The Graphic* in 1891

MATTHEW NICHOLAS
THE COXSWAIN
OF THE
BOAT

Mayon Cottage (now renamed) where Richard Nicholas lived.
Elisabeth Stanbrook

Reliefs

The reliefs continued to be undertaken by the Nicholas family. In 1890, possibly upon the retirement of Matthew Nicholas, the offer of Richard Nicholas for 'boat-work' was accepted on the following terms: trips for stores - £4 10s per quarter; trips for reliefs - £12 12s per quarter; extra trips £1 1s each; allowance for looking after the boat - £1 1s per quarter. In September 1897 an additional boat hire allowance of £12 a year for conveying oil and stores to the lighthouse was sanctioned. Richard Nicholas lived at Mayon Cottage with his wife and family.

As with everything else, the boat needed occasional repairs. In 1892 this was undertaken by J. W. Legg for £18 10s 8d and in 1894 repairs cost £11. The relief boat endured many turbulent trips so these repairs were not surprising. In November 1894 a very rough relief was undertaken. PK John Watson and AK Roberts managed to be hoisted up onto the lighthouse, but Supernumerary Assistant Jackson fell into the sea - a 'boiling surf' - while trying to leave. Fortunately he had on his life-jacket and was rescued, but he was 'dragged on board the boat well nigh exhausted, and terribly frightened'. The relief boat became so covered in foam that it disappeared from the coast-guard's view at Pedn-mên-du, above Sennen, and they thought the boat had been swamped.

Shipwrecks

Despite the raised light of the 1870s lighthouse, there were still occasional shipwrecks. On 30 September 1891, during a terrific gale, the schooner *Annie Davis* of Carmarthen got into difficulties off the Longships, and the keepers fired signals to the mainland indicating that help was needed. The storm was so severe that seven of the lifeboat crew of thirteen refused to go out, and the lifeboat had to be manned mostly by volunteers, much to the disgust of the local community. In treacherous seas the boat went to the rescue of the schooner, but by the time it arrived on the scene it was nowhere to be seen. At about midnight a violent storm came in and it was impossible to get back to Sennen, so they had to go to St Ives, getting in at about 4am. In all they had been at sea for eight hours. The schooner was later found abandoned in the Bristol Channel, all crew gone, into smaller boats, and presumed drowned.

In February 1896 the London barque *Scottish Knight* hit the Longships. It was carrying a cargo of nitrates from Queenstown for Leith. After being towed by a steamer it foundered at Three Stone Oar. All crew were saved.

Perhaps the most famous shipwreck was on 9 November 1898 at five minutes to midnight when the rock on which the Longships stands was struck by the cargo steamer *SS Blue Jacket*. It had been en route from Plymouth Sound to Cardiff. A newspaper report revealed that Captain Thompson had been on the bridge until 11.20pm and then left the ship in charge of Mr Sinclair who left his

S.S. Blue Jacket wrecked on the Longships rocks. Courtesy Cornish Studies Library

The old lifeboat house which Trinity House took over in 1896.
Elisabeth Stanbrook

post for a few minutes to go downstairs and consult with the Captain. The man at the wheel noticed they were heading for the Longships rocks and telegraphed to the engine room for full speed astern, but to no avail. The ship struck a shelving reef and she was forced right up under the lighthouse. 'There were three shocks, and the steamer's bottom was torn away to the engine-room.' As the sea did not gain access to the after-holds, the crew were able to converse with the lighthouse keepers above them. Rockets and signal guns were fired, and the Sennen lifeboat was launched. All the crew, and the Captain's wife, were rescued and taken back to Sennen. The remains of the *Blue Jacket* were sold by public tender to Messrs R. Thomas, J. Chenhalls and J. Brean for £27.

A new lifeboat station was opened in 1896 at Sennen Cove on the site of the present one. Trinity House then took over the old lifeboat house, complete with a cockloft, for its own use. The building is now a shop.

In 1896 the PK at Longships lighthouse was John Ball. He wrote a memoir of his time on the Rock, and described it as one of the most dangerous rocks in the service, more lives having been lost here than at all of the other rock lighthouses put together '... there seems to be a kind of tidal wave that comes in occasionally, and when one least expects it.' Ball discusses landing stores:

> ...it then depends on the state of the tide and direction of the wind, we have a Jib we put up at the Nth. Pt. and also the Pollon [Pollard] when it is a bit rough, and then all stores, water coals and oil are hoisted on to the top rock, ready to be carried up into the house, and when it is too rough to step from the boat on to the landings, the keepers when we are relieving are hoisted up in the same way each man being provided with a lifejacket, to be used on all occasions when landing or embarking.'

Ball also talked of the Longships being more advanced than other rock stations regarding communications via Morse code and semaphore. 'Great strides have been made, we are now able to hold communication with the Wolf Rock a distance of nearly 8 miles, we also signal to dwellings ashore every night and day so are now able to get all the latest news both for Service and for private use... the old style of signalling by hoisting flags ...are nearly obsolete.'

CHAPTER SEVEN

Lighting and fog signal

A new system of lighting – an incandescent oil burner (IOB) – and fog signal were installed in 1904. The IOB had been invented by Arthur Kitson in 1901 and gave a brightness of 150 candles per square inch, trebling the power of wick burner lights. It had been developed for lighthouse use by Thomas Matthews, Trinity House's then Engineer-in-Chief, and was a petroleum vapour burner using pressurised light mineral oil fuel with the mantle. It also used much less oil.

In about 1908 author J. Harris Stone joined the supply boat taking out a consignment of oil from Sennen Cove to the Longships. The oil 'was in iron drums of about 18 inches by 10 inches, with two iron handles on the top' amounting to 50 in total. At the lighthouse 'the drums of oil are hoisted up by a crane from above five at a time, tied together, and a rope passing through the handles at the tops.' The drums had to be taken up 49 internal iron steps to the oil store where they were decanted into eight large upright cans each bearing the words '145 gallons'. He was impressed with the lantern room, and admired the 4,000 candle power apparatus. This was described as an 'angry red glare' by one visitor.

On 1 December 1923 a Hood petroleum vapour burner was installed at the Longships lighthouse. As the mantle was larger in

Plan of rhe incandescent oil burner of 1904. *Courtesy Trinity House*

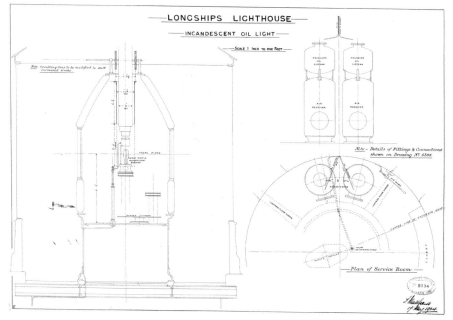

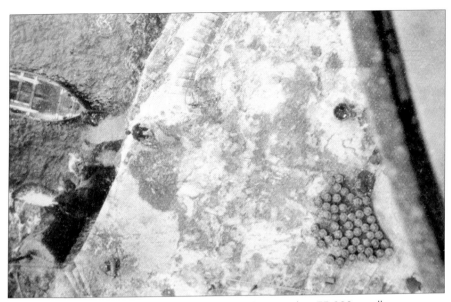

The oil drums delivered to the lighthouse in 1908.
J. Harris Stone

size, the light it gave out was increased to 75,000 candle power.

The interior of the lighthouse was also painted periodically, and a record for 1924 reveals that it was painted light and dark blue set off with a band or two of green.

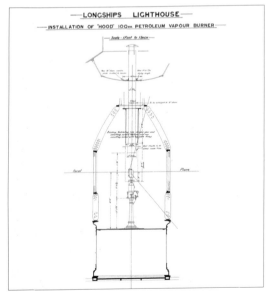

Drawing of the Hood petroleum vapour burner.
Courtesy Trinity House

Communications

The Cornishman of May 1905 reveals that there was no wireless communication between Longships and shore. The keepers had special signalling lamps for clear nights only, plus their explosive rockets, and semaphore for day use. Two years later, the PK noted that the 'AKs are very expert at semaphoring, practising daily with their families at the dwellings, but that the present flashing lamp is scarcely powerful enough for communication with the Wolf.' Eight years later, in 1913, the Board of Trade asked Trinity House to assess the suitability of the Longships and Wolf Rock lighthouses and Seven Stones light vessel stations for installation of wireless telegraphy. But it was rejected for the Longships.

By December 1938 *The Cornishman* indicated that the Longships still had no radio telephonic communication, even though some other lighthouses did. The keepers relied upon Morse lamps and semaphore. Prompted by a health emergency of a keeper, and long reliefs, MP Alec Beechman asked the Board of Trade why this was so. In early 1939 Board of Trade's President, Mr Oliver Stanley said that there were no plans to install radio telephones at Longships, but they were experimenting at the Wolf with low-power radio telephone sets on loan from the Marconi Company.

Acetylene signalling lamps were installed, and changes were made to the rocket signals used to summon assistance for vessels in distress in April 1937. The signals fired by day were now to be identical to those given in darkness; i.e. firing light rockets in addition to sound (explosive) rockets. Also, the Distant Signal – a ball over a square flag – was to be exhibited at all rock stations on all occasions by day when distress signals were made. The balls were five feet in diameter and would be sent to all rock lighthouses.

A keeper sending a semaphore message from the lighthouse door.
Courtesy Trinity House

Shipwrecks and the rocket house

Another shipping disaster had, in November 1901, come perilously close to the Longships. The Penzance schooner *Mary James*, carrying copper ore and road stone to Swansea, foundered when she hit a nasty squall. Her rigging gave way and the masts went overboard. All crew were saved by the Sennen lifeboat as the stricken vessel was swept towards the Longships. Wreckage eventually washed up along the coast near St Just.

On 15 March 1905 another shipping tragedy occurred when the 2,000 ton, full-rigged sailing ship *Khyber* was wrecked off Porthgwarra, near Land's End, with the loss of 23 men. She was

The 1906 rocket apparatus house built on land at Mayon Farm. *Bryan Roberts Collection*

observed from the Longships and the keepers sent signals to shore, but by the time horses from three-quarters of a mile away at Mayon Farm had been taken down to the cove for the rocket apparatus, established there in 1869, the ship had disappeared. There was a detailed inquest into this wreck, and it was recommended that the rocket apparatus house be moved to land at Mayon Farm, near the horses, thus saving valuable time.

The Board of Trade agreed to build the concrete-floored brick and slate rocket apparatus house and it was completed in October 1906. Records show that it was occupied and held on lease by Trinity House from 1 January 1906 for 40 years and was probably used to store their own lighthouse explosive rockets. The Coastguard Service also had use of this building for their rocket apparatus, and it survives today.

On 30 November 1919, a shipwreck occurred on the Longships reef. H. M. motor launch 378 was one of several launches accompanying destroyers *Urchin* and *Ursula* on their way from Queensland to Southampton when around Land's End they encountered a very strong gale and heavy sea. The weather was so rough that the lighthouse was nearly obscured. The engine of 378 became disabled and the launch met with 'total destruction' on the rocks. First Lieut Herbertson RNVR was drowned, but the eight remaining passengers, including the Captain, were saved by the Sennen lifeboat crew, for which they received vellum and medals from the RNLI for gallant conduct.

The former rocket apparatus house today.
Elisabeth Stanbrook

CHAPTER EIGHT

A new breakwater

The need for a new breakwater at Sennen Cove was made all the more pertinent by the loss of the *Khyber* as launching the lifeboat from Sennen in bad weather had been nearly impossible. In December 1906 a Provisional Order was made to the Board of Trade for a breakwater and separate slip at Sennen Cove, with the removal of the old breakwater and slip; the Engineer was William Tregarthen Douglass.

The old breakwater in early 1908.
J. Harris Stone

In August 1907 Royal Assent was received, and Trinity House gave £150 towards its cost because all supplies and reliefs took place from Sennen Cove.

Mr Arthur Carkeek of Redruth was awarded the building contract in March 1908, and work started in late June. On Wednesday 22 July the 'memorial stone' was laid at a special ceremony and, once finished, the new breakwater was widely appreciated.

It was not until 1923 that the new 20-foot wide slip was built by Messrs Triggs Bros of Newlyn. It was finished in October, and

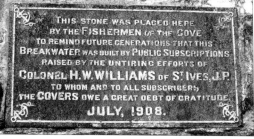

The memorial stone laid in July 1908.
Elisabeth Stanbrook

The new breakwater.
Elisabeth Stanbrook

they were then awarded the contract for building a wall 60 feet long and 20 feet high and three feet wide connecting the breakwater and slipway on one side, and infilling the gap between the slipway and the wharf wall on the other for £125. The wall, completed on 26 November, was to cause problems for the relief boat, as seen below.

The slip built in 1923.
Elisabeth Stanbrook

The keepers

On his visit to the lighthouse in c.1908 J. Harris Stone noted a banjo, a bagatelle table and a gramophone used by the keepers for recreation purposes. He also commented on their consumption of occasional 'bird-pie'. The powerful light attracted birds to the gallery and, dazed by the light, a keeper could step out onto the platform 'to pick off as many birds as he wants' and wring their necks.

Assistant Keeper W. J. Clay succumbed to 'heat disease' in June 1913 'and is incapable of exertion.' He was taken off the lighthouse as soon as a relief could be undertaken. Mrs A. Trezise, AK Clay's daughter, remembered when he and PK W. Harvey Odden were on the lighthouse for four months and 20 days due to bad weather. When brought ashore the boatmen had to help them both as they were so weak from lack of food. They had lived on bully beef and ships biscuits and baking powder bread. The boatmen even had to hire a pony and jingle to take the men home.

During the Great War physically fit men could not join Trinity House lighthouse service in place of joining up for active service, but those not fit for active service could be considered. There were no major incidents for the Longships during the war, but German U-boats did invade the waters from time to time.

Another tragedy occurred at the lighthouse on 8 May 1917. AK Christopher (Chris) Nicholas fell 110 feet to his death on the rocks below from the lantern gallery while cleaning the glass. Aged 44, he had lived in one of the dwellings with his wife and children. PK Charles Thomas thought he may not have secured the ladder properly. Chris's ghost is said to haunt the lighthouse, and the spot where he landed is known as 'Chris's Landing'.

In 1919 PK Le Gallais took up his post. That year Trinity House found the Longships efficient but not in good order. 'The paintwork was dull and the quarters untidy... The spare bedding is uncovered and dirty.'

Some of the keepers were finding themselves at the Longships for many years running and many requested a move to a shore station. Given all these requests, in autumn 1931, Trinity House decided it could be made a 3-year station, excluding relief time.

On the death of King George V on 20 January 1936 all Trinity House personnel, including the lighthouse keepers, were required when in uniform or wearing their great coats, to wear 'the regulation band of Black crepe, 2½ inches wide, round the left arm above the elbow.' The service ensign had to be flown at half mast every day until sunset on Tuesday 28 January, the day of his funeral.

Keepers' pay was raised at regular intervals, for example, in May 1936 AKs now earned between £99 10s to £137 per annum, depending on age and service years, and PKs now earned between £150 to £156 per annum, depending on age and service years.

There were occasional problems with lighthouse cleanliness as already seen. On 29 December 1938 Trinity House issued a circular that to prevent vermin in wooden bunks at Rock lighthouses, the bedrooms were to periodically be 'cleaned out thoroughly and completely'. All woodwork and walls were to be washed down with water mixed with a suitable quantity of disinfectant to prevent any accumulation of dust etc. 'At all times, immediately after a bed has been slept in, the mattresses are to be turned back for ventilation and airing, and the blankets and sheets are to be aired and folded.'

Reliefs

Richard Nicholas, the Trinity House relief boatman, was provided with a new boat in 1905 which was 'much appreciated.' Regular repairs were necessary and by July 1920 the sails of the boat were condemned and, in 1923, a new and 'very good' relief boat was

The relief carried out by rowing boat.
Elisabeth Stanbrook Collection

ITS A LONG PULL TO LONGSHIPS. 1 2.

Supplies delivered to the lighthouse in *Boy James*, 1935. *Courtesy Morrab Library*

Keepers and boat crew set off in *Boy James* from Sennen for the lighthouse. At the rear is James Howard Nicholas with Jim Nicholas (owner of the boat) in front of him. *Bryan Roberts Collection*

provided. By 1931 the first motor relief boat, *Boy James*, had replaced the rowing boat and, in the late 1940s, a new diesel boat replaced this one.

Roller truckles for launching the relief boat at Sennen Cove were supplied in 1920, and a hand winch was used for hauling the relief boat out of the water after each trip. The RNLI used another nearby winch for their lifeboat (until they obtained a motor one in the early 1920s), and Trinity House sometimes had the use of this when theirs was undergoing repairs.

The wall by the slip, built in 1923, was causing problems for relief boatman Richard Nicholas as stores had to be lowered by hand from the sea wall to the breakwater before loading – a distance of 16 to 18 feet. His repeated requests for a small crane fell on deaf ears. By now reliefs were 56 days on and 28 days ashore.

Terrific storms continued to affect the reliefs. In January 1924 a relief took place which ended a very long incarceration in the

lighthouse. Not only were the lighthouse keepers imprisoned in the granite tower, but two mechanics, Messrs Skelton and Gregory, who were undertaking repairs begun in November 1923, were also trapped. Keeper W. Jordan had been on duty the longest as he had begun his stint on 1 October. The others had been out there for about 11 weeks. With an extra two mouths to feed, the only food left was some flour and tinned meat, a victualling relief only having been managed once in treacherous conditions. It was one of the roughest reliefs ever experienced by the men, and one keeper said that never before had he been relieved in such terrible weather; so bad was it, in fact, that the two mechanics refused to risk their lives in the attempt to reach the relief boat, and remained on the lighthouse with the

The wall which caused problems for the relief boatman.
Elisabeth Stanbrook

newcomers. They were relieved the following day. Sea sickness did not help those involved in this dramatic event. Tributes were paid to Richard Nicholas jnr and his relief crew, John Penrose, R. R. Nicholas, Walter Nicholas and Ernest George who displayed remarkable skill in such a turbulent sea.

On Christmas Day 1924 several keepers were marooned on the lighthouse because of bad weather. They were due to be relieved on 19 December but were unable to be taken off until early January 1925.

Ten years later, in January 1935, three lighthouse keepers were relieved by Mr J. Nicholas after spending many weeks on the tower due to bad weather. AK P. J. Wood had been on the lighthouse for 11 weeks (his relief had been due on 19 December), while AKs V. A. Hughes and S. G. Davies had been there for seven weeks. It was described as the worst Christmas on the lighthouse for five years, and it was especially so for AK Davies as his mother died while he was trapped there. All they had left was bully-beef Christmas dinner with peas and potatoes and Christmas pudding.

For the first time, victualling the lighthouse took place from

The Trinity House relief boat from an old postcard.
Elisabeth Stanbrook Collection

Waiting in *Boy James* for calmer seas to rescue sick Keeper Griffiths. A photographer, Mr Richards, is in the life jacket, 14 December 1938.
Courtesy Morrab Library

Trinity House vessel *Satellite* due to rough sea conditions in early February 1938.

When *Satellite* had approached as near as safety would permit, she dropped anchor, and lowered her boat – an able craft. Into this were placed watertight canisters filled with potatoes, beef, bacon, cigarettes, yeast, butter, cheese, tea, sugar, fish and chocolate. The boat was then taken as close as it could get to the landing place, rocking and rolling all the time, and several rockets were fired attached to which were over 150 fathoms of line. A keeper managed to catch one of the lines and secure it while clutching the post at the end of the landing stage and getting soaked by high waves and spray. The canisters were then hauled over successfully. Shortly afterwards, a relief was undertaken and PK Clemens, AKs Moore and Burgess were very glad to reach home.

One of the keepers was taken very ill on the lighthouse in December 1938. PK Godfrey said, 'In all my experience of a lighthouse keeper, this is the most anxious time I have ever had. Horsley, the other keeper, found Griffiths unconscious on the lamproom floor. Getting him down the steep staircase into a lower room was a very difficult job. I thought once or twice Mr Griffiths was going to die.' Various Morse code messages went back and forth between the keepers and a doctor on the mainland. There was a certain amount of difficulty in getting the keeper into the relief boat, but it was achieved albeit with his suitcase falling into the sea. It was retrieved soaked through. Back at Sennen he was taken to the cottage of James Nicholas from where he regained his strength.

In May 1934 Richard Nicholas of Sennen died. He had been a Trinity House relief boatman for the Longships for over 50 years before he retired. He had also worked as a lighthouse keeper.

CHAPTER NINE

The Second World War

In August 1940 all manned lighthouses were supplied with ARP equipment for dealing with incendiary bombs. Two months later the Engineer-in-Chief recommended that Radio Telephony at Longships, Bishop Rock, Wolf Rock and Round Island lighthouses be approved, including for communication through Land's End Coast Radio Station, but with a supplementary shore station at Sennen's Coastguard Lookout.

Additional keepers were employed at the Longships in case enemy action rendered a keeper incapacitated. It took more than two keepers to operate the landing winch, so four were to be on duty and two on shore for the reliefs.

Local memory recalls that the lighthouse continued to be lit and that the Luftwaffe used it as a marker to begin their journey for air raid missions.

In 1942 MoD Transport announced that Rock lighthouse keepers could be paid a War Risk Allowance while proceeding to and from lighthouses by sea in a Trinity House tender or other vessel approved by the minister.

Life on the lighthouse

By now, the lighthouse had become a popular attraction from Land's End, the presence of keepers installed in the tower adding to the interest people took.

The lighthouse had become a popular attraction. Elisabeth Stanbrook Collection

The Longships Lighthouse from Lands End

The relief boat *Bonnie Lad* motors out to the Longships lighthouse.
Bryan Roberts Collection

An account of life on the lighthouse was written during the mid-twentieth century which gives an insight into conditions for the keepers. Trinity House supplied the keepers with a box of books which could be changed on relief. Hobbies were undertaken such as mat making, carpentry and model making, and one keeper with a mechanical aptitude made an electric clock.

The duties at the Longships were similar to other rock stations:

The forenoon is taken up with general duties such as preparing the light for that night's exhibition, cleaning the lens, lantern and service room. The cleaning of the various rooms, brass-work etc is allotted to different days. The day is divided into four watches, 4am – noon; noon - 8pm; 8pm – midnight; midnight - 4am. In the event of fog the Keeper on duty in the lantern calls out the man who he relieved to take over fog watch. When he, in turn, is relieved he takes over for fog watch, so in foggy weather it means an extra watch has to be kept, which is cut out of ones "watch below". During the daytime the keeper on watch works the fog signal himself.

One Keeper is cook for the day, he prepares dinner and cleans the kitchen and bedroom, the keepers take that job in turns so it works out for each man every third day. Each keeper makes his own bread though, some are better than others at the job but each man thinks he makes the best bread.

One Christmas I spent on the rock the dinner was quite different to

Bird's eye view of the relief.
Bryan Roberts Collection

The relief underway from *Bonnie Lad.*
Bryan Roberts Collection

Seven-year-old Margaret Drew singing carols transmitted from the cockpit of the Penlee lifeboat.
Courtesy Penlee Gallery

that which we had looked forward to. We had been overdue for a couple of weeks owing to bad weather, and our supplies had got very low. Christmas Eve came around and no sign of the relief taking place so we searched our cupboards for stuff to make a Christmas dinner; amongst us we found some currants and a few raisins, spice and luckily some suet. That pudding was made and boiled twelve hours and was really good. We had for our first course a tin of Bully Beef, some ships biscuits soaked and then fried with slices of beef on top garnished with haricot beans.

On 12 June 1947 Keeper Barnes lost his life while on duty, and the following November another keeper was dismissed the service on 19 November 'for refusing to proceed to duty.' Also that month an irregular running of the lighthouse occurred and a SAK was cautioned 'to carry out his duties in a proper manner in future'.

Bad weather in December 1949 meant that the keepers could not be relieved for Christmas Day. However, they and other keepers in Cornish and Welsh lighthouses were treated to a broadcast of a seven-year-old girl from Mousehole, Margaret Drew, singing carols transmitted from the cockpit of the Penlee lifeboat; her father was the lifeboat's Engineer. At 11am she sang *Away in a Manger* and *Once in Royal David's City* followed by more carols sung by members of the Mousehole male choir who had also crowded into the cockpit. Margaret had sung carols for the keepers the Christmas before as well.

Keeper A. J. Lane recalled being on duty over Christmas 1953 on the Longships when he found himself cook on Christmas Day. He produced mock-turtle soup and Christmas pudding. That July the lighthouse had been fitted with an 'Electrolux Type' L150 refrigerator. At 10.30 am each lighthouse or vessel in the area sang a carol; the one from the Longships was *Silent Night*.

The only sink on the lighthouse was in the kitchen. This had two taps; one produced rainwater from storage tanks underneath the lantern gallery. 'Rain that fell on the lantern roof dissolved first the seagull droppings, then the salt-rime, then the chemical film deposited by the fog-signal charges, before passing the interesting solution down the astragals to flow across the pitch-covered gallery to the outside gutter cut into the topmost course of the granite, and thence to the storage tank.' The other tap supplied drinking water from a small header tank in the kitchen which was topped up by a hand pump from cisterns in the base of the tower.

A new lighthouse keeper temporarily joined those already stationed at the Longships on 15 November 1956. Bob Eley presented himself at the home of the elderly relief boatman-cum-fisherman in Sennen where his wife gave him a huge lunch of mixed boiled fish. Afterwards, the boatman and his son undertook the relief which, as Mr Eley recollected, 'was in fact, quite a difficult and skilled undertaking, taking the boat into the swirling waters among rocks. It being my first time of joining a tower by rope the boatman took great care that I did everything safely.'

Mr Eley continued, 'A few words sent over the lighthouse radio that day were answered by the keeper's wife waving a pair of flags outside the door of their cottage. Her first words were about an important message for me. My dear wife had that day given birth to our second daughter.' It was to be nine weeks before he saw his baby daughter as reliefs lasted for two months then. In the 1970s it was changed to one month on, one month off.

Mr Eley also remembered the kindness shown to the keepers by the relief boatmen. 'Frequently they would depart from the grounds where they were fishing to deliver papers, letters etc (and often a couple of nice crabs) to the Longships Lighthouse. I have heard such stories of much the same at other rock stations too.'

Another lighthouse keeper, Handel Bluer, was posted to the Longships on 24 June 1959 until his transfer to Nash Point, Glamorgan on 4 November 1963. He remembers the system of radio communications as being rather primitive, being a very early two-valved ex-military 'Man-Pack'; one valve was a triode, the other a pentode. The power used was a glass two-volt accumulator for heating the filaments and a 120-volt 'Dri-Pack' battery for the

The Tol-Pedn-Penwith Coastguard Station was to become a Base Station for R/T Communications with the Longships.
Elisabeth Stanbrook

high tension supply. The power output was less than five watts, and the aerial had been erected in a makeshift manner resulting in poor efficiency. As the Coast Radio Station (Land's End Radio) was at St Just, Trinity House considered the system as 'adequate for purpose' – providing that it was not raining! Operation from transmit to receive, and vice versa, involved a changeover switch to select the right 'crystal' to transmit, while retuning the receiver involved moving the dial to a coloured line painted on the body of the set. These were red for 2182 khz emergency and 'calling' channel; black for 1841 khz Land's End Radio's working channel; and blue for 1652 khz for the Trinity House working frequency. Exchanges were not quick.

It was during Handel Bluer's time that the use of the white-painted doorway for semaphore purposes came to an end. In 1961 he had taken out a transistorised 'domestic' receiver which incorporated the 'trawler-band' of 1.6 mhz – 4 mhz. This enabled a duplex telephone style method of communication, and keeper's wives acquired these 'trawler-band' receivers for use in the dwellings. At the lighthouse a telescope was mounted in the Service Room so that keepers could talk via the trawler-band, and see their wives' replies by semaphore, without having to go outside. 'One day, coming up to Christmas, with a westerly gale blowing, my wife opened the window to "talk" to me. The result? All the garlands strung across the ceiling were blown down and the Christmas tree felled!!' On his next shore leave, Mr Bluer bought an ex-RAF Aldis lamp and built a mains converter so that she could communicate through the window, having first taught her Morse code. Mr Bluer also recalled that his wife always signed off with 'I LUV YOU'. One evening, 'a passing Irish and Continental line steamer – in line of sight – also received this "farewell" and gave what passed for a wolf whistle on the ship's siren!'

During 1965 Trinity House decided upon a programme of modernisation for 1967 at the Longships lighthouse. The light was to be electrified and have a character of isophase (equal periods of light and dark) every 10 seconds, visible for at least 16 miles. The explosive fog signal was to be replaced by a tyfon fog signal with a character of one blast of 1.5 seconds duration every 15 seconds. The Tol-Pedn-Penwith Coastguard Station at Gwennap Head was to become a Base Station for R/T Communications with the Longships and other lighthouses in the area.

On 28 February 1966, due to appalling weather which prevented supplies of oil by boat, the Longships became one of the first lighthouses to have deliveries of oil by helicopter. An RAF Mk. 10 Whirlwind helicopter flew in to Sennen Cove car park and picked up a supply of foam rubber mattresses for padding the lantern glass against mishap. It then flew in 300 gallons of oil in six trips, landing them on the gallery while keeping the rotor blades clear of the radio

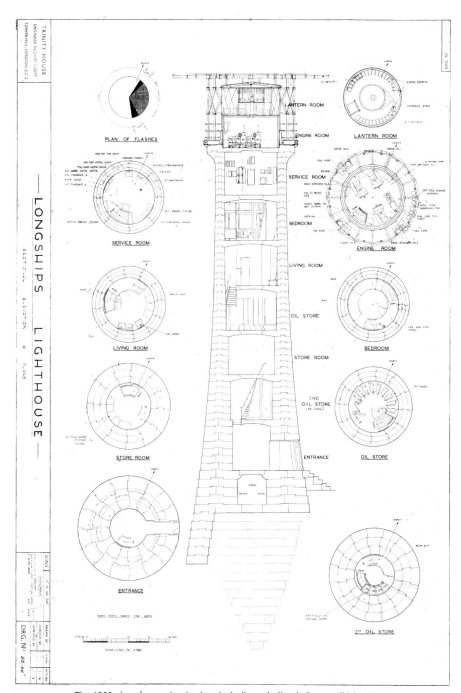

The 1966 plans for modernisation, including a helipad. *Courtesy Trinity House*

aerial and wind indicator, controlling the whole operation through endless sea spray from the turbulent water below.

Keepers

Gordon Partridge went to the Longships for his first off-shore lighthouse in 1976 for one month, as a Supernumerary Assistant. In his book he describes the interior of the lighthouse during the mid-1970s:

> 'Longships Lighthouse had eight floors including the base door at almost sea level, yet within that structure there were only two rooms for domestic use; most space being given over to Engine Room, Fuel and other Stores, whilst the toilet was down adjacent to the base. ...The bedroom had only two metres of free floor space at best; fortunately the skills of the Victorian builders had made best use of space beneath the bunks by building in lockers and drawers in a really inspiring way; their woodwork was superb.
>
> 'In the kitchen, ...when watching television, it was not possible to open the door without at least one other person having to move his chair!'

The Penlee lifeboat tragedy on 19 December 1981, with the loss of lifeboat *Solomon Browne*, the 1,400 ton coaster *Union Star* and all those on board the two vessels, is one of the more tragic shipwrecks to occur here in living memory. The *Union Star* suffered engine failure near the Wolf Rock and drifted helplessly towards the rocks at Land's End. The Longships lighthouse keepers could have only watched helplessly as the drama unfolded.

CHAPTER TEN

Modernisation

Just prior to the modernisation works of 1967, a large crane post had to be installed on the Pollard landing so that the heavy equipment could be off-loaded from the boats. A German compressor was used to drill the seven-foot deep hole needed to anchor in the post. The work took over two months. The installation of the crane post itself was extremely difficult and exhausting work, largely due to its size and weight.

While undertaking the modernisation work, there was insufficient accommodation in the lighthouse while the mechanics were there. So two of the keepers were temporarily withdrawn and the necessary watch was maintained by the remaining keeper or a mechanic. The old oil lighting mechanism and the lenses of the light were taken away, and two floors were formed in the space created. The electric generators were installed in the lower one and the new optic in the top one. In the meantime a temporary light and fog signal had to be in place before the work began.

The lantern floor being modernised to take the new optic. *Courtesy Association of Lighthouse Keepers*

Making cement for the works. *Courtesy Association of Lighthouse Keepers*

On the night of 3 October, the new permanent light, with a first order dioptric lens, was exhibited from about 6.30pm to 8.10pm for test purposes prior to the new light being permanently exhibited on 1 November 1967.

On 6 December the new permanent Supertyfon fog horn came into operation. Successful listening trials of the new signal were on 7 December.

The next few years saw the usual repairs and replacements on the Longships lighthouse including new fuel tanks and VHF/Radio Telephone installation in 1968 which involved thermic lancing of the tower for the electric cables.

The new agreement with Mr James Howard Nicholas, the relief contractor, had been approved in October 1965. By April 1968 relief rates were revised from £20 to £30 for a relief trip; from £10 to £15 for an unsuccessful trip; and waiting time from nil to £7 10s per hour (up to two hours). But relations between Nicholas and Trinity House began to become strained, possibly over the inevitability of relief boat services becoming redundant with the introduction of helicopter reliefs on the horizon. In December 1973 Nicholas was no longer

Buckets of cement reaching the gallery. *Courtesy Association of Lighthouse Keepers*

Working the winch for the equipment. *Courtesy Association of Lighthouse Keepers*

prepared to carry out the Longships relief etc and recommended an alternative boatman, the owner of *Castle Boy*.

The Nicholas family had relieved the Longships lighthouse for over 100 years, starting with Matthew Nicholas for the Wyatt structure. This was, indeed, the end of an era.

The first experimental helicopter reliefs took place at West Coast lighthouses on 19-22 June 1969. Their overall success satisfied the Engineer-in-Chief, Mr Ian C. Clingan, who, in November 1973, requested approval to progress work on the helicopter pad at the Longships as a matter of urgency. The Corporation was in favour of a 27-foot diameter helipad and in December placed an order with Non-Corrosive Metal Products Ltd for aluminium decking material at a cost of approximately £2,700 in advance of the inevitable sanction being obtained for this work.

The helipad

The helipad, which was to revolutionise the relief and supplies to the Longships lighthouse, was built in 1974. The foundation work was undertaken by Soil Mechanics Ltd for £2,777, while construction on the lighthouse was carried out by Scott Wilson Group plc, a global design and engineering consultancy for the built and natural environments.

To carry out the reliefs Trinity House contracted two Bolkow 105D twin-engine helicopters from Management Aviation Ltd, Bourn, Cambridge (to become Bond Air Services in 1984), which could carry four passengers. The lighthouse relief exchanged three keepers with their 270 kgs of gear and provisions for their monthly turn of duty. Reliefs were rarely delayed as the helicopters could fly in up to storm force 10 or 55 knots, although fog could cause a few disruptions. The Sennen helicopter base was built at the Sennen dwellings but reliefs also took place from Penzance and later St Just where there is a helipad exclusively for Trinity House.

After years of using the Bolkow 105D helicoptors changes in relief and servicing requirements saw Trinity House move to a new contractor. They signed a new Helicopter Services five-year contract with Police Aviation Services (PAS), effective from 1 December 2010, to supply an IFR (instrument flight rules) rated MD 902 Explorer for 32 weeks of each year.

These helicopters have seating for a pilot, flight engineer and up to six passengers. The passenger seats can be removed or replaced so cabin cargo requirements can be easily accommodated. The under-slung payload is up to one tonne, and can carry life raft, emergency floats and supplementary fuel tank amongst other items.

In 2014 the General Lighthouse Authority entered into a seven-year contract (to start on 1 December 2015) with PDG Helicopters to provide this service for Trinity House, The Commissioners of Irish Lights and The Commissioners of Northern Lighthouses under a single contract.

On 7 October 2015 PDG took ownership of a new EC135 helicopter, with call sign G-GLAA, bought for this purpose.

Relief helicopter at the Sennen dwellings.
Mary Evans Picture Library/Andrew Besley

The helicopter G-BATC on the Longships lighthouse helideck during a relief.
Courtesy Christopher Nicholson

Automation

Automation of the Longships lighthouse started in 1987 and work continued until its completion in 1988. This saw the end of an era as 193 years of the light being lit by keepers gave way to modern methods.

From 1996 the Longships lighthouse has been monitored and controlled from the Trinity House Operations and Planning Centre at Harwich.

The solar panels fitted in 2005.
Courtesy Trinity House

Always looking for ways to be more cost effective, Trinity House sanctioned the conversion from diesel to solar power on the Longships lighthouse in 2005. The BBC gave an interesting insight into the work involved. In February Dave Steer and his colleagues flew out for the job which would last five months, living out there two weeks at a time.

Their task was to disconnect and remove the old diesel powered system and install the solar power system in its place. All the old fuel tanks had to be removed but they could not be taken up the stairs to the helipad so the crew had to manoeuvre them out of a window.

The solar panels were installed early on in the conversion but it was months before they were working. These panels, which power

Built to withstand the worst of storms.
Tim Stevens

giant batteries, were flown out to the lighthouse, an exercise initially hampered by thick fog.

The men had to face another arduous job with the installation of the new back-up generator. It was one of the more dangerous aspects of the whole exercise.

Living on the lighthouse was a new experience for the workmen, as it must have been throughout the lighthouse's history. All their fresh water was flown over, and 'it can also seem like a long way down to that bathroom in the middle of the night so the men have "pee pots"'.

Three years later, on Tuesday 29 April 2008, Karen Richards and Mo Coulson from Cornwall were sponsored to spend two nights on the Longships lighthouse to raise money for the charity Children on the Edge, set up by Anita Roddick of Body Shop.

There is a Trinity House Depot at St Just, Cornwall from where equipment is sorted and placed into an underslung cargo net to be flown underneath the helicopter for delivery to the lighthouse.

Today the light source is a 3kw lamp giving a white and red isophase every ten seconds (light 5 seconds, eclipse 5 seconds) with a 14,400 intensity. The range of light is 15 nautical miles. The fog warning apparatus is one blast every 10 seconds.

The Longships lighthouse has now become part of the Land's End experience, a magnet for thousands of visitors to the area each year, and in all weathers. It stands as a reminder of the tenacity of the ill-fated Lieut Henry Smith and his vision, and the importance of Trinity House who bought and maintained the lighthouse, before replacing it with the graceful structure we see today. It undergoes regular maintenance by Trinity House, and its light has kept shipping and mariners safe in this treacherous piece of dramatic coastline.

Looking past Enys Dodnan and the Armed Knight to the Longships lighthouse.
Elisabeth Stanbrook

ACKNOWLEDGEMENTS

I am greatly indebted to all the following associations, libraries, record offices and individuals for their invaluable help, including images: Alison Abbiss; Angove Collection; Association of Lighthouse Keepers (ALK); Handel Bluer; Bryan Roberts Collection; Cornish Studies Library, Redruth; Cornwall Record Office, Truro; Devon Heritage Centre, Exeter; former Devon News Service, courtesy ALK; Bob Eley; Ken & Teresa Howe; Institution of Civil Engineers; London Metropolitan Library; Mary Evans Agency/Andrew Besley; Tony Millett; Morrab Library, Penzance; The National Archives; Christopher Nicholson; Penlee Gallery, Penzance; Peter Puddiphat; Tim Stevens; Corporation of Trinity House.

And lastly, but by no means least, I would like to say a special thank you to Tom Greeves for his interest and support throughout my research, Neil Jones, Trinity House Archivist, who provided and gave permission for the use of Trinity House plans and photographs; and Gerry Douglas-Sherwood of the Association of Lighthouse Keepers for providing information and images.

SELECT BIBLIOGRAPHY

Adams, Andrew & Woodman, Richard *Light Upon the Waters – The History of Trinity House 1514 – 2014* The Corporation of Trinity House 2013

Anon *A Guide to the Mounts Bay and the Land's End* W. Phillips, London 1824

Cobb, James F *The Watchers on the Longships* Wells Gardner, Darton & Co 1876

Douglas-Sherwood, Gerry *A Glossary of Lighthouse Service Terminology* Association of Lighthouse Keepers 2000

Everard, Cyril, Msc Fgs Hon Frgs, *The Isles Of Scilly and The Channel Islands: `Bench-Mark' Hydrographic and Geodetic Surveys 1689-1980 Volume Two* Queen Mary, University of London 2004

Jones, Ted *Stranded on the Longships* Merlin Books Ltd 1991

Lane, A J *It Was Fun While It Lasted* Whittles Publishing 2009 edn

Nicholson, Christopher *Rock Lighthouses of Britain* Patrick Stephens 1983 and Whittles Publishing 2006

Noall, Cyril *Cornish Lights and Shipwrecks* D. Bradford Barton Ltd 1968

Noall, Cyril & Farr, Grahame *Wreck and Rescue Round the Cornish Coast: II: The Story of the Land's End Lifeboats* D. Bradford Barton Ltd 1965

Partridge, Gordon *Hands That Made Lights Work – A Lighthouse Keeper's Essay* AuthorHouse UK Ltd 2010

Report of the Commissioners appointed to enquire into the Condition and Management of Lights, Buoys, and Beacons 1861 Vols I & II. (Vol XXV – 2793)

Stanier, Peter *South West Granite – A History of the Granite Industry in Cornwall & Devon* Cornish Hillside Publications 1999

Stevenson, Robert (edited by Stevenson, D Alan) *English Lighthouse Tours 1801 1813 1818* Thomas Nelson and Sons Ltd 1946

Stone, J. Harris *England's Riviera* Kegan Paul, Trench, Trubner & Co Ltd 1912

Williams, Thomas *Life of Sir James Nicholas Douglass FRS* Longmans Green & Co 1900

Woodman, R. & Wilson, J. *The Lighthouses of Trinity House* Thomas Reed Publications 2002

Periodicals etc
Cornish Telegraph, The various
Cornishman, The various
Flash & *Horizon* Trinity House, various
Lamp Association of Lighthouse Keepers, various
Minutes of the Proceedings of The Institution of Civil Engineers, various
Royal Cornwall Gazette, various
Trewman's Exeter Flying Post, various

Websites
www.alk.org.uk;
www.trinityhouse.co.uk
www.lighthousekeepers.co.uk
www.bbc.co.uk/insideout/southwest/series9/week_five.shtml
www.cornishmemory.com